William Alexander Thomson

An Essay on Production, Money And Government

William Alexander Thomson

An Essay on Production, Money And Government

ISBN/EAN: 9783744724241

Printed in Europe, USA, Canada, Australia, Japan

Cover: Foto ©Thomas Meinert / pixelio.de

More available books at **www.hansebooks.com**

AN ESSAY

ON

PRODUCTION,

MONEY AND GOVERNMENT;

IN WHICH

The Principle of a Natural Law is Advanced and Explained,

WHEREBY

CREDIT, DEBT, TAXATION, TARIFFS, AND INTEREST ON MONEY WILL
BE ABOLISHED ; AND NATIONAL DEBT AND THE CURRENT
EXPENSES OF GOVERNMENT WILL BE PAID IN GOLD.

———————————

By WILLIAM ALEXANDER THOMSON.

BUFFALO:
PRINTING HOUSE OF WHEELER, MATTHEWS & WARREN,
COMMERCIAL ADVERTISER BUILDINGS.
1863.

PREFACE.

READER, in the present essay I have, in the briefest way, attempted to draw attention to some of the greatest principles of human life, and I have undertaken to show the necessary relation which is designed to exist between the functions and duty of man and certain laws of nature, which have been since the beginning of time.

Life, with its aims and purposes, appears to me as gathering its results into a profitless and puny issue. The individual seems lost in mankind. Chains have been riveted out of material transactions, binding him hand and foot. It is held to be a virtue to labor to the exclusion of all thought and human enjoyment in obtaining the present mere material necessities, and to provide for repose in the decline of life. The bounding and generous ideality of youth is frowned down. The earnest desire for wisdom and understanding of manhood's prime is frozen in the bud, that no exalted idea may interfere in the endeavor to obtain an imaginary and uncertain repose in after life — a period at which man, whose mind has been devoted to mere pecuniary gain, is past usefulness to God, the world or himself.

The principles of life which I advance will, if acted upon, totally and absolutely reverse much that now holds, and ensure a degree of *easiness* in all life's pursuits, that will warrant the discovery and application of many Laws of Nature to man's well-being, now perfectly unknown.

The material advantages which will follow the application of this

Law, are really wonderful as compared with wretched darkness and universal disappointment in the system of Credit and Credit Money. Herein I foresee the obstacle to a ready appreciation of my enunciations in the present Essay, because Man, before he can see Truth, must divest himself of Error.

Truth requires to be examined philosophically and not by comparison with, or reference to, a present condition of things, based on false data. Almost all mankind are the slaves of rules, systems, ideas, which they have never examined; and yet if a truth is advanced, they immediately fall back upon these stereotyped conceptions, of which they really know nothing, as a reason why they should earnestly oppose any new thought advanced, and which new thought, if it is a great Truth, they never will understand, unless they can first divest themselves of an adherence to false laws now holding them in abject bondage and ignorance.

It was Lord Bacon that said, "Read not to believe, nor to contradict, but to weigh and consider."

WM. A. THOMSON.

Fort Erie, Canada, February, 1863.

DECLARATION.

The natural method of producing MONEY, is for banks and individuals to pay gold, which is the "measure of money," into a Government "Bureau of Production," at the current price, which shall be issued instantly, by the Government, in ounce pieces, in discharging the present expenses of governing the nation.

The depositors will receive "acknowledgments," in convenient amounts, from one dollar and upwards, which shall become "evidences" of money, and retain value through all time, within the duration of the productive capacity of the nation, and will be IRREDEEMABLE and a LEGAL TENDER.

The application of the gold by the Government will indoctrinate this money in all property within the nation, making it intrinsically and permanently valuable ; and the products of the system will be as follows:

1st. A full money, equal to moving the greatest producing capacity of the nation; and which can never fluctuate in value.

2d. *Production* will then *create demand*, when over-production will be impossible, and every thing produced will instantly find a ready money sale.

3d. Taxation and Tariffs will cease at once, as unnecessary and pernicious.

4th. Debtor and Creditor will be obsolete terms, after ten years.

5th. All *products* will be much cheaper, and *fixed properties* having a producing power will be more valuable.

6th. Within ten years the debts of all governments will have been paid, without taxation or tariffs, in gold; no matter how great such national debts may be.

7th. In ten years after this system has been at work, POVERTY will be unknown, unless accompanied by incurable vice, or physical incapacity.

8th. Happiness and intellectual activity will replace discontent and ignorance.

9th. Men will work longer, live longer, and die better.

10th. Individuality will be ensured to the individual, without which condition there is no thought growth. There is not a "free man" in a credit country, or where the spiritual man is subject to "material" obligations.

11th. The government, without taxation or tariffs, will possess gold to pay the expenses of itself, and, also, the expenses of a national character of the minor municipalities always.

12th. Mankind, as compared with present progress, will in twenty years be advanced centuries on the highway of intellectual, moral and spiritual growth, and of human happiness and comfort.

13th. After ten years, the supply and demand of money being then equal, and by this law to remain so, money can never thereafter be an article of profit in itself; it will be a "motor" of production of material substances, out of which, only, will *profit* arise. It will also be the exchanger of products.

Argument.

Were crude physical labor, without mind power, the only means of production, every thing would be for local supply, and no more being in demand, barter would meet the limited condition. In this state of society man could never rise to moral intellectuality.

It is coeval with the national formation, that the mind begins to dawn, as a power, in the world's economy, instantly comprehending the requirement for system in production and government; perceiving that productions were valueless without protection, and feeling, that out of unassisted physical labor, the expense of governing would crush the desired advancement. And thus, the Intellectual, growing slowly, through many ages, has been drawing onwards to a condition of harmony with Natural Law *in the production of material substances.*

Properties would be valueless in a savage condition of life, which under civilized nationality are wealth: that only being wealth which has within itself a productive quality, and as it produces. The national condition can only be obtained by the acquiescence, in matters of general import, of the whole people, forming, or intending to form, a nation. If a nation is thrown back into anarchy, or barbarism, the value departs from its properties, for, production ceasing, there could be no wealth.

Thus, it is apparent, that every thing of a national character depends, for its continued value, on the wholesome working and preservation of the national system. And, as national compact is a natural law, then, every thing that can permanently strengthen and solidify the same, should possess the attributes of eternal justice, benevolence and truth. Credit, which is the present great co-motor to the mind (and, therefore, while it holds sway, lies at the root of the first principle of national formation, which is the production of material substances; out of which production, relatively, if unshackled, there would follow intellectual, moral and spiritual growth), has the very contrary of these attributes, for its characteristics are injustice, cruelty and fraud; and its fruits are moral degradation and national decay.

There becomes, therefore, an imperative necessity for a *natural money*, to underlie, and finally obliterate credit, Nevertheless, we can not part with the one until we get the other.

Property outside of Nation being valueless, which inside is valuable, the means of making it more and more valuable is in increasing its productive capacity, and in giving protection to property and person. Now, if this protection were given, without taking any "value" from the citizen, would it not be reasonable to admit, that whoever paid the needful values for such governmental security and protection, thus leaving all the "means" of the citizen with himself, to create further production (not otherwise possible to such an extent), should have an interest in all the properties of the nation, to the amount of his advances?

And, if these advances (made from year to year for ever) were not repayable, were not a loan, nor to be in any way a lien, either for principal or interest, upon the property of the nation, would it not be right to say, that the party making these advances held an equitable ownership, and should possess a transferable "acknowledgment," relative in amount with such advances, in all the (now called) assessable property, acquired, or to be acquired, by the citizen?

This condition of affairs would only be *just* and philosophical, if it were beneficial and profitable. Thus, it would require that such advances should greatly increase the general value of fixed properties, and also the ability of the citizen, to further increase their productive power; while at the same time there was full assurance of protection of government, in person and property.

It is through just such a process, foreshadowing such results, that I elsewhere show how, in strict accordance with the requirements of human society and progress, and of natural law, a true money can be obtained.

THE LAW.

The desideratum in the matter of money, is to provide for an ample circulation, free from fluctuation, and always equal in amount to the fullest natural demand of production, in material substances.

From the want of a knowledge of the law of money, as intended by nature, all the accumulations of the production of labor, in material substances, are resolved into fixed properties. A *true* money is requisite, to combine the varied powers of mankind, mentally and physically, to ensure a full and multiplied production, out of fixed properties. The process of credit, which has emanated out of man's ignorance and necessities, has come to a "dead-lock," swallowed up in the vastness of the fixed properties, which it has aided in producing; and which fixed properties are descending in the scale of true productive value (which is the value of all property — property having within itself a productive capacity, being the only WEALTH), by the incapacity of the moral, man, to increase credit co-equally with the requirements of increased properties.

All that is now called money, *is not money*, not even gold and silver; but all paper "promises to pay," called money, are a mere credit, and the gold and silver, instead of being used as a " measure of money," are degraded, as a basis for the support of credit.

I proceed to propound the law of money, as evidenced in the past and present history of man's necessities, in his primary field of labor, in material substances, And I am impelled to this utterance of the " truth within," by the conception, that all of mankind's intellectual and moral growth, all of present happiness or misery, all of human woe, beggary and vice, or of virtue, comfort and goodness, will be RELATIVE with the possession of true or false laws, governing the fundamental laboratory of man's existence, the production of material substances.

The atmosphere, by co-creation, is in affinity with the earth. "Money" should likewise be in harmony with fixed properties, by both coming out of the net profits already earned; thereby giving the same surety of result to the work of the "mind motor," that the atmosphere secures to the decree of the God of nature, in reproduction on the earth. And, as the atmosphere can only return upon the earth by virtue of common affinities, resulting from co-production, so a true money and fixed properties should come out of the same crucible of net profits already earned; that both being the products of labor in material substances, may naturally re-affiliate with each other in their separate characters of floating and fixed properties, causing ceaseless multiplication of production.

Money is an invisible substance, represented by some visible sign, be it paper or metal. Such signs are not themselves money, but the "evidences" thereof. Human law is required to regulate the "evidences," but the law of nature ordains the money.

The *first* purpose of money is as a CO-MOTOR, subordinate to the mind of man, which is the prime motor, in bringing the varied powers and faculties of mankind to bear in national compact, to the greatest possible advantage upon material productions.

The *second* purpose of money, is to exchange the products of industry and to socialize all the nations into one, in the Eye of the Universe. Therefore, a true money of any nation will be esteemed permanently valuable, and its paper "evidences" will pass current, the world over.

The natural boundary of a nation is in its industrial economy, and in the equality of its parts in harmonizing with a common centre. Under the true law of production and its money, countries will sooner or later come together to make one nation, or separate to make two nations, as they are now naturally, or unnaturally joined, or disjoined.

Out of the instinct of nature, individuals have been resolved into nations of mankind, whence a governmental necessity at once presented itself to protect one from the other; to secure the fruits of production to the producer, and to preserve the national compact against the aggression of all other nations. This again created a demand for services, or something to pay services of government; and, clearly *all* must contribute, directly or indirectly, towards this object; and herein arose taxation. Even taxation, as the world increased, could not be paid in material substances, and thus, at the present day, men have first to work unaided to gain possession, expensively, of "evidences of credit" called money, and when they have earned it, the government wants are the first to be supplied. And thus, this sham money, which would have *trebled* itself as a *motor* in a year, if left in the hands of the producer, has gone into the hands of the government where it will make no production of material substances.

No natural law impoverishes. All natural laws are beneficent and productive. Taxation, poverty, vice and misery are clearly related. The eternal justice ignores them all.

We have under natural destiny formed nations, and instantly government, with its expenses, follows; and as soon as industry takes root, we discover the necessity for a money, to harmonize the combined individual functions into national power, in economizing and increasing productive capacity.

Nation, government, production, are no more intimately related than the expenses of governing, and the money "motor" of production in material substances. A natural relation binds them all.

As the world now appears, there is no avenue by which any portion of the net profits of production in material substances can be made into money! So all net profits must go into fixed properties, such as farms, machinery, mines, houses; and they, in turn, become the basis of a credit to move themselves. One law makes fixed properties, and another makes the present money (?). They are thoroughly antagonistic to each other, and the result is, partially valueless properties, dear products and down-trodden humanity. The present money never moves production, it only exchanges products.

Credit is a base money, and is, thus far, within natural law, otherwise it could not be even temporarily operative.

To institute a true money, and to displace credit, gold must cease as the basis of the present credit system of bank notes, and be established as the "measure" of "money." Whenever the net profits in the production of material substances earn gold, authorize it to be lodged in a bureau of production of the nation, and an "acknowl-edgment" or "acknowledgments," to be a legal tender and irredeemable, be granted in return by the said bureau.

The Gold thus lodged in the bureau of production by banks or individuals, as often as they wanted paper "evidences" of money, the government shall stamp in ounce pieces, and issue in payment of daily expenses of governing the nation, and in paying government debts where any exist.

The net profits, in the production of material substances, will never fail to earn as much gold as there will be money motor wanted, to vitalize all the fixed properties to be moved, to further production.

The Acknowledgments granted for the gold lodged in the bureau of production, will become "evidences of money" from the application of the gold, through the medium of the government, in the defraying the expenses of the nation, and in rendering taxation, tariffs, and all other imposts, for ever unnecessary.

The Gold received by the bureau of production becomes thoroughly indoctrinated in the properties of the nation, by thus paying all the expenses thereof. And the acknowledgments are thereby resolved into "evidences" of an imperishable and unfluctuating money.

A Money! Implanted in all the properties of the nation, because the vitality and value of fixed properties (productive capacity being the only test of value) will rest on the continued existence, usefulness and quantity of the "evidences" as a "motor of production;" while the money will equally depend upon the productive value of the fixed properties for its character and quantity; and both on the perpetuation of the national compact. The one valueless without the other, and naturally intended to be coexistent and equal in duration.

It will be required of the government, that the gold which the bureau of production receives, and melts into one-ounce pieces at the mint, with the stamp of purity and date thereon, be paid out without delay, from the various disbursing stations, in payment of governmental debts and expenses. And if the receipts are more than the chief government requires, that the minor municipalities, according to census, shall receive monthly proportions of such surplus. First, that simultaneously with the issuing of "evidences" of money against it, the gold shall go at once where it will fulfill the duty which gives the enduring value, within the national existence, to the money, namely: to the payment of government services in behalf of the property and person of the citizen. Secondly, that the government may obtain the value of the day, for the gold, at which it was taken. And, thirdly, because, under unshackled production, every thing is in activity, and the gold, being the "measure of money," should be where it can be instantly reëarned, by the ever-recurring net profits of production in material substances.

Gold, or any other substance of material value, can not be even an evidence of money, because it would then have two natures in conflict. It would fluctuate as a merchantable value; and it could not possibly pay the expenses (and prevent taxation) of the nation, and circulate as an "evidence" of money. For how could the government get it to perform the *double* transaction which the creation of a natural money does?

A true "evidence" of money—money being invisible, and yet positively valuable—requires to be in itself *valueless*. Paper answers that purpose, and can carry its history and origin on its face to the conscience and understanding of the world.

Bankers, with commissions on the footings of accounts for their remuneration, will be the natural link between the bureau of production (which I propose that every government shall establish) and the earners and owners of the net profits of material substances.

All gold will continually revert to the banks; it can not stay in circulation where a true money exists. The gold will reach the banks through depositors; and when depositors draw checks against their accounts, paper money will be wanted; the banker's duty, therefore, will require his having a supply of such money on hand, and thus the gold must be sent in constantly to the bureau of production for the obtaining of what we now call "currency," but which in this case will be *real money.* And real, because of the application of the gold, through the government, to the defraying of the expenses of the nation, and thereby obliterating taxation, tariffs and every other drain now made upon industry.

Until the "relative" in supply and demand, between money and properties, under this law, is first established, there being *now* no money, and all "properties," the greatest proportion of net profits will flow into money, gradually displacing all credits and false money; thus an amount of money, equal to about one-half of the present productive properties of a nation, will be created, and hence an equal sum in gold will be paid, through the bureau of production, within a cycle of about ten years. And as some

B

fixed properties must be added, by the nature of industry, within the said ten years, an amount, equal to about the half of said additional fixed properties, will also be wanted in money, further increasing the gold paid into the bureau. When the equilibrium has arrived between money and properties, after a period of ten years, and all national debts have then been paid off, as they will be through natural consequence, it will happen, from that forward, that the additional money annually wanted to move the additional fixed properties, annually created, will flow evenly, governed by an eternal law, which invariably regulates the "fitness of things." And the gold thus annually paid into the bureau of production will be found equal to meeting, thereafter, all the annual charges of the nation, and of such expenses of the minor municipalities as are of a national character.

I discover a "relative" in natural law, between the additional money wanted annually by unshackled production (after supply and demand are once equal, at the end of ten years) to meet the additional fixed properties annually earned, and the quantity of gold needed to defray all national governing.

I repeat, these "acknowledgments," by the application of the gold, becoming "evidences" of money (money being itself invisible), are irredeemable and a legal tender, having no redemption, because paid for when obtained, thus representing profits previously earned. A thing to be redeemed, apparently, requires something more valuable than itself. But true money, indoctrinated in all the property of the nation, and having vitality, through the productiveness which it aids in creating, and being, under unshackled production, the only invariable value, can find nothing in existence, of ample value, in sufficient quantity to exchange it. Certainly, neither gold nor silver can meet the case, they being limited in quantity, and fluctuating, merchantable substances.

No accumulation of gold, by the government, will be justifiable; for, gold being the "measure of money," it is important that all of the "measure" shall be continually within the reach of the acquiring power of the net profits of production, in material substances. Nor, are the "acknowledgments" granted, truly "evidences" of money, until the application of the gold is made; for, gold in government vaults would be mere merchandise, and thus the "acknowledgments" would only be "evidences" of *merchandise*, and not of money.

No superabundance, however, of gold ounces, in circulation or in bank vaults, will ever over-increase the paper "acknowledgments;" for, although all the gold will be earned, over and over again, and placed in bank deposit by "net profits" of production, in material substances, yet, only so much gold will pass into the Bureau of Production as there are "acknowledgments" needed by the demand of fixed properties, within their producing ability.

The intelligent mind, which carefully studies this subject, will discover, under the machinery of this money creation, that production, net profits, additional money, increased fixed properties (wealth), can not avoid growing "relatively." And with unshackled industry, which will then hold, that it will be impossible to disproportion any thing.

The lodgments of gold with the bureau of production will not decrease the power of continually lodging more; every ounce paid in being immediately issued by the Gov-

ernment, and re-obtained by the banks, who will keep
sending it in to the bureau just as often as they have
occasion for paper evidences of money, to meet, through
their customers, the demand in the production of material
substances. And it will be unprofitable to send it in
faster than paper money is needed, as gold, in superabundance, in a nation, can be exported to a probable profit;
but money having no productive or material value WITHIN
itself, and not being an article of merchandise, consequently
bearing no profit, will be, in surplus, totally valueless as
an investment.

The money under this law will never fluctuate in value—
it will rule all values. The degree of value in all fixed
producing properties of the nation will depend upon the
relative amount of money afloat. When supply and demand are equal, then property will be at its highest degree
of productive capacity, and consequently of standard value.
And under a true law creating unshackled production, the
amount of money can never be in excess; because the gold
has to be earned before the money can be created, and the
money must be required before gold will be given for it.

A natural law regulates itself, and it is no true law
which needs human weakness to say: "Thus far shalt
thou go, and no farther." Once industry is unshackled,
by the enunciation of a true money, so that PRODUCTION
forthwith CREATES DEMAND—when over-production will be an
impossibility, and when every thing produced will find a
ready sale for money—then the declaration of the French
economist, M. Say, will be applicable: wherein all that
a government has to do with national industry and its
money, and with Domestic or Foreign Commerce, is "to
certify a fact and to prevent a fraud."

MONEY is to fixed properties as the atmosphere is to the earth. As the air is to the lungs. An invisible substance to a material substance. Atmosphere is just as real as Earth. True money is just as real as machinery, or farms, or food. Money is the floating element of fixed capital in material substances.

There is no money now in existence. Real money is incompressible by legislation or otherwise. A stunted metal circulation may be a safe medium of EXCHANGE in countries where there are no paper notes, but still it is not money. And where bank notes, or government credit issues, are in force, then all is credit, even gold and silver; the one being a mere sustainer of the other.

Credit crushes, debt destroys; whilst production, aided by a NATURAL MONEY, will expand the natural powers of the whole man, swelling general wealth, human happiness and intellectual capacity many hundred-fold.

The net profits in production of material substances are only obtained after deducting the consumption of all the people of the nation, productive and non-productive. It is these net profits which now all go into additional fixed properties, that would partly go into irredeemable money, if a money channel existed.

There are no additions to *wealth* in the world, except by the net profits of production in material substances, and yet this production supports *all* before net profits are ascertained. This being so, the great act now required in the onward drama of life, is to *unshackle* this great element of productive wealth; and just as the productive power increases, so much and no more does every other branch of human life advance. And it may be said, that "relatively" with the productive capacity of a people, will ever be their intellectual, moral and spiritual growth. It is therefore presumable that man's present degree of wisdom and understanding is very far below par.

Unshackle production in material substances, which can only be gained by developing a natural, and, consequently, true money, and you will have advanced mankind, by many centuries, toward grander thoughts and greater happiness.

Although the paper "acknowledgments," or evidences of money, under the law now proposed, will never depreciate or fluctuate in value, and we have an established line of values of all things now existing to commence upon; yet gold, taken by the bureau of production to-day at $17 per ounce, and issued in payment of government expenses at the same rate, may afterwards fall to $15 or $10, or rise to $20 or $25 per ounce. This will make no difference to any one, for it will only rise and fall as a merchantable commodity, measured by the true money in existence; although becoming the measure itself of further money, at the reduced or increased price which true money will rule it at in the market of the day. The bureau of production will, on the price of the day, give "acknowledgments" for gold without any reference to what it had been taken in or paid out at, previously. The Government, in paying out gold in ounces, will stamp no value on the same; the current value will be known to giver and receiver, and as Government will not retain gold on hand, the nation will be sure to receive value, in services, equal to the face of the acknowledgments granted.

Under a natural money, with all the cost of credit abolished, all products will be greatly reduced in the cost of production, and greatly increased in quantity—demand will be (exactly) equally increased—and gold will rule relatively in its cheapness and increase of production, but will have no effect on a true natural money, which is itself intrinsically valuable, rules all and never varies.

I have said that the first purpose of money is, as a co-motor to the mind of man, which is the chief motor in the production of material substances. Therefore, man had already, without the aid of money, made some crude strides in production, otherwise there never could have originated "a money." But, with the first excess of production over consumption, the initiation of a money was possible, and in nature necessary.

If the creation of what we call wealth is a natural law, —and that it is a natural law is evident from the fact that in the production of material substances, and as the capacity of production increases, so does the moral and intellectual being called man relatively develop himself in the appreciation of human happiness and in the service of the universe,—therefore, the knowledge of what money really is, and how to apply it, is a prime necessity.

The mind of man can not act outside of natural law, yet it is the decree of destiny that he must work out all truths for himself by the exercise of the functions of mind implanted within him. The spirit of truth, although always within us, succumbs to error, and will apparently lie dormant for ages, unless the individual man, in a happy moment, sees error in its deformity and calls upon Truth to awake. Meantime our vital necessities, blindly knocking at the door of natural law, succeed in creating systems, which, though erroneous, are yet within natural law, else such systems would be impossibilities. Nevertheless, false conceptions, however long they may last in action, ensure present misfortune and ultimate destruction.

Money is now a thing of profit, and yet of itself produces nothing. No producer can obtain it until he has long labored without its aid in acquiring capital and credit, and then, and only then, can he *borrow* it in limited quantity and at a large profit to the lender; and it is only as a temporary motor that he can then rely upon it. No production can be cheap and very advancing with such a trammel; and thus we find that the rule of life is, that the majority fail in obtaining competence or happiness, and that a vast percentage of mankind sink into beggary and desolation.

Money, not first earned in the workshop or on the farm, only gets there in paying for something produced without the aid of money. What millions fail to reach a first loan! lost to themselves, to the world and to God's service. And this is the action of what is now called money. It is apparent that all production is now the effect of the mind motor and social credit, and that what is now called money is the *agent of commerce*, in being a mere *exchanger* of products after they are produced, and never the co-motor of production.

Thus, if on any occasion such money is rapidly increased, it adds but little to the productive power, simply increasing the *exchanging* ability. This surplus of exchanging medium, without corresponding production, will immediately raise the price of products. Then it is that production, seeking for *credit* to supply a co-motor, tries to meet the apparent increase in demand; and, production being wonderful in its power, and the money issue under present system being, even in excess, limited, production will rapidly fill the market, overtopping the exchanging medium and ensuring a speedy collapse and certain disaster to all.

False money, issued even by a government, no matter how large the quantity, can never keep pace for any length of time .with production, and all increased *profits*, made under excessive issues of false money, can only go into fixed properties, inasmuch as *net profits must go into something not yet created.* The bank notes, government notes, gold and silver, are already earned and owned by somebody, and can not be increased by changing hands; therefore the certainty of a crash, in ten-fold degree, is unavoidable, because properties being now too much for all the credit in existence, the disparity will be greatly multiplied by the addition of property from profits, while taxation increasing, will be reducing the motive power and ready means within the present system. Thus, when the collapse happens, apart from the increase of human wretchedness that will arise, there will be a depreciation of fixed properties just equal to the amount of social credit withdrawn; and in a great nation, this will count thousands in subtraction for the hundreds of additional wealth realized under the inflation. It being borne in mind that fixed properties are the only *wealth*, valued by what they produce, and as they produce, and, as the present system makes *demand create production*, and the last part of the family to get over a collapse is the commercial *credit* giving branch, which credit now moves demand, the great disaster and its prolonged effects on fixed properties may be comprehended.

Bank or government notes not arising out of net profits of production, but issuing against something yet to be earned, do not move (and they contract the profits) production. But the obtaining of the "wherewith" by production to pay a profit on the bank notes, or, all the principal in taxation of the government notes, reduces the productive capacity of a nation annually about three times the amount thus paid for profit in the one case, and for principal in the other.

It is a mistake that war expenditures, if confined to the citizens, do not impoverish as much as if to foreigners. As much productive power is displaced, when the citizen produces for the government consumption, as would produce enough, or perhaps more than enough, in other productions, to pay foreigners for the articles and services wanted by the government.

Individual gain may be at the expense of other individual loss. The only gain to the nation is in the *aggregate net profits* of the whole people in the production of material substances. The other branches of life's labor are all dependencies and charges on the production of material substances, prospering only as production prospers.

A money capital, in the production of material substances, moves annually about three times its amount; therefore, in wars, which are all sheer waste, the first direct loss is treble amount of the expenditure; which, in a great war and under a false system of credit and taxation, may be a death blow to a nation, but which under a natural law of money, would have merely the effect of making, for a time, less fixed properties and more money. But making the existing properties produce more, and thereby increasing their value, equal to the amount of additional net profits, put into money, to pay the war waste.

The amount of debt, in every shape, in existence, is the deficiency in the amount of money which ought to be in circulation to make supply and demand equal, under natural law. And nature, permitting no vacuum to remain, and debt being a vacuum, has so arranged the functions, necessities and thoughts of mankind, that, moving under a natural law of money, whereby *production creates demand,* a national debt, however large, will, by the instinctive creation of additional money, first earned in the production of material substances, be discharged without Government commands or legislative enactments. Nor will the domestic economy of the people, under a true money, be affected by war, in comfort, happiness or progress, beyond the sorrow for life lost, and in the amount of mind motor and physical labor extinguished.

I again repeat, that the *first principle* in a natural money, is as a MOTOR of production in material substances; and, I would add, that there can be no legitimate "exchanger" of products which has not first, by aiding in production, as a motor, been the gauge of values in the producing.

Under the present system, when there is a flush of paper issues and credits, making active demand, there is limited supply of products to meet it; but when by aid of such temporary flush, production becomes active and the markets are filled, it is found that the credit has collapsed and the paper issues are in deficiency and therefore no sufficiency of demand; thus high and low prices alternating, and no general profit in either case. It is one step forward and another backward, always destructive to every attempt of production to work up to its capacity. Whatever increase in material wealth goes forward under such a system, as compared to nothing, may seem considerable, but as compared with what it ought to be, is as next to nothing.

The law of money now propounded will enable *production to make its own money.* From the small smithy to

the great manufactory; from the little garden to the great
farm; in short, in every spot where material production
makes profits, a portion will be converted into money;
not by exchanging for a money now in existence, for that
would not increase money, *but by investing it in additional
and new money obtained through the governmental requirements of the national compact.* And the money will be
exactly where it was earned, instantly, without expense,
loss of time or debt, ready to stimulate the additional fixed
properties, simultaneously developed, thus ensuring un-
checked multiplication of production at greatly reduced cost,
with a never-failing demand. Money and production being
limited under a natural law, where *production creates demand* ONLY by capacity of the producing power, no mortal
intervention, individual or governmental, will be admissible
in the law of production. Government is merely a *channel*
through which the "net profits" pass gold and receive
"acknowledgments," which, from the application of the
gold which the government is *instructed to make*, the conscience and reason of the nation are enabled to declare the
"acknowledgments" true "evidences" of a perfect money,
co-existent with the productive capacity of the nation, and
as vital to live out political disasters, as are the properties
and the individuals within the bounds of the nation.

What is now called money is only credit, for it is
predicated to be made valuable on profits *yet to be earned.*
The money which I advance is made by the net profits
already earned. True money being real and intrinsically
valuable, needs no redemption. All credits are "promises
to pay," and they must be redeemable in something of
value *and which has yet to be produced.*

Productive capacity being the measure of value of

properties, and money being the co-motor in production, the properties and money would be valueless but for each other. Therefore, money and properties should grow, relatively, in required proportions, for ever, within the duration of a nation. The same money in existence to-day, without the possibility of change or depreciation, to be afloat a hundred or a thousand years hence. As an exchanger of products the paper evidences of such a money (money being invisible) will be current the world over, above either gold or silver.

Every nation has within itself the element of a full money, from its formation. All that has been heretofore borrowed from one nation by another has been ruinous to both borrower and lender, *for under a true money law all the money made in a nation will be required to move production, out of the net profits of which, only, is* WEALTH *made;* and the only property that *is* wealth is fixed property having a productive power within it. In the acquiring of such wealth there need be no limit in any nation.

It is a striking illustration, in a nation having *money to lend,* that in the lending nation a false (credit) money, like the present, does not assimulate in further production, showing that it is merely an *exchanger,* a "thing of commerce," and therefore it goes abroad at the expense of limited production of fixed properties; by its export causing dear products and limited value in properties at home.

A nation having money to lend, under present false systems, will increase its poor and its poor-houses, relatively, as it increases its lending capacity. Inevitable destiny.

A nation which borrows money from another, under

present false system, indicates too large a domain, or too much fixed properties, with too limited a power to make full capacity of production. Such a nation will not make "abject poor," like the other nation, but it will make universal misery, precarious fortunes, disease and shortened life amongst its inhabitants.

From the extreme magnitude of transactions, and difference in principle of exchange, under this system, the evidences of money will represent sums from one dollar to one hundred thousand dollars. Ten, twenty and fifty thousand dollar "evidences" will be then as common as fifty and one hundred dollar notes are now. Although thousands of millions will be in circulation, the quantity of separate "evidences" will be less proportionably.

As paper is perishable, and this money is to endure always, the bureau of production will *renew* all "paper evidences" of five or ten years issue. But this and all other machinery of the department being merely mechanical and office work, need not cumber this philosophical and practical, though brief, annunciation of a true money, and consequently of unshackled production.

The production of material substances, and its money motor, under true natural law, will regulate all other branches of life, and the "money motor" will be the proper "exchanger" of all productions. As is the standard high or low in the capacity of production in material substances within a nation, so are all the people in comfort, happiness, intellectuality and virtue. There is no escape from the "relative" within the sphere of natural laws. Under the present system, ~~when~~ properties grow faster than even the credit motors (there being no money), proportionably, because man can not expand the degree of credit as fast as

net profits make additional properties, therefore production
is far below what would be its capacity under unshackled
industry, equally on the broad American continent, in North
America and the Canadas, and in France and England.
Although the aspect is different in America and Europe;
which difference it is unnecessary and perhaps impolitic to
discuss herein.

It must be true beyond all question, however strange
it may appear, that mankind, in the aggregate, are reced-
ing, in intellectuality, morality, happiness and individual
wealth. The few may be growing rich and learned (learn-
ing is neither wisdom nor understanding), but it is only
an exception to prove the rule.

Credit has reached a limit, at which it should be sup-
planted by a *true* money, which would totally underlie it,
within the first ten years of its action, and raise mankind
heavenward, in worldly condition. Otherwise, there will be
a period of retrogression, dark and cruel, in the history of
the world.

REFLECTIONS.

Credit is the inexorable tyrant of the nineteenth century. It has, in the absence of the natural motor of production, been of service in increasing, to a certain extent, the productions of material substances. Without "money," in proper quantity, which is the true co-motor, the mind of man being the motor, and without the system of credit, the only productions would have been those of unassisted physical labor. Mankind generally would then have been somewhat like the Indians in civilization.

Credit begets debt, and debt is alike abhorrent to God and Man, because it dwarfs individuality, and is foreign to the natural law of production. It sends millions to misery and destruction, and prepares few for God's service. Credit is the "skeleton in the closet" of present civilization.

When Robert Burns composed the following verse, "credit" must have been the "lordling" to which he alluded.

> "If I'm designed yon lordling's slave —
> By nature's law designed,
> Why was an independent wish
> E'er planted in my mind ?
> If not, why am I subject to
> His cruelty or scorn ?
> Or why has man the will and POWER
> To make his fellows mourn."

C

For every purpose of man's life there is a natural law. Man's conditions were made to accord with laws, already established. And man can only *truly* prosper as he discovers and acts up to these laws. When man loses the consciousness of his own individuality, within which all truth must come, if it comes at all for him, by having allowed his mind to fall a victim to stereotyped systems, rules and habits, which have imperceptibly enthralled the mass of mortals, then his power to distinguish between the true and the false is nearly gone.

The economy of the universal kingdom requires of man, in this world, a knowledge of the laws of nature, under which his Being is planted; and the discovery of these laws, in physical, mental, moral and spiritual degree, and the exercise of them afterward, are the only conditions under which he can contribute to the strengthening and enlarging of the moral powers of the universe—to the perfecting of his happiness in the present life, or, to an intelligent hope of an immortal individual exaltation hereafter. Studying the economy of man's existence from this stand-point, he has, most certainly, very much to un-learn.

No branch of life's action, except the production of material substances, requires any notice whatever here, beyond saying that out of the production of material substances, of which the mind of man is *the* "motor," and "credit," under a false system, and "money" under a true system, is the "co-motor,"—all other phases of society have their relative advancement.

Under the base system of credit, production is limited by demand, and hence, general advancement is retarded; but, under a condition of unshackled production, which can

only be with a true money, the whole family of man will
advance rapidly in physical happiness, and in intellectual,
moral and spiritual grandeur; and vice, beggary, sorrow,
and wretchedness will relatively decrease. There is not a
doubt of the soundness of these premises. And just as
the production of material substances (I do not use the
term labor, of Adam Smith—it is too limited in its signifi-
cance) approaches a high or low standard, so is all up or
down for mankind.

Nor does this claim in favor of industry disturb the
fact that man is born with a brain organism, capable of
producing every thought, sentiment and propensity which
characterizes the individual called man. But thoughts are
not born, they are an *after-creation*; and only to the extent
that a system is true and free, under which the man lives,
do thoughts grow toward truths, and Truth is immortal!

I repeat, that a system of unshackled industry, which
can only hold where a true, and, consequently, unlimited
money is developed (unlimited, except by the demand of
the net profits of production), is essential to the salvation of
man's present happiness and future state.

Under a true system, with a proper money, production
creates demand equal to its greatest capacity. Nature has
so ordered the various capacities and necessities for different pursuits, productive and non-productive, *that no people,
under a natural money, can produce more, in the aggregate,
than they can consume.* If too much of one or more
articles is produced, then a proportionate deficiency in other
articles wanted by that people, will hold.

Gold established through an uncomprehended law of
nature, first as an "evidence" of money, and since as the
"basis" of money, of most nations, and yet not to be

found in all, forbids the possibility of exclusiveness by any nation as against all the others.

And thus, through the non-universality of gold, and the irregularity under differences of climate, in the quantity of general products, there follows that commercial cementation of one nation with another, by which all the earth shall be as "one people" in the Eye of the Universe. And hereby, the articles produced in surplus are exported and exchanged for other articles, to meet what was manufactured in too little quantity in the exporting nation.

Under the true principle,—only possible with a natural money, viz: Of "production creating demand," and over-production of material substances, or of money, being alike impossible,—then production will hold the first, and commerce the second rank, in the world's economy. Commerce, now, by being the credit regulator, rules production, and is a besom of destruction to human happiness and intellectual growth.

Credit, banking, and all other institutions of life, are approaches to natural law. "Whatever is, is right," up to the point where it can be bettered. Credit has prepared mankind, through a century or two of fierce and unhappy activity, for a true money.

Credit has sent millions off the earth, unreclaimed and lost, for every one that it has strengthened and exalted in moral intellectuality.

Credit, like the silk worm, has created so large a cocoon (fixed properties), that, as the worm dies when its cocoon is finished, so credit is unable to put productive life into the vastness of its property creations, and thus property generally is deficient in value, because deficient in productiveness from want of money, to cause it to fully produce; and, credit being of human growth, not coming out of the net profits, already earned, of material substances, can not keep pace, or steadiness with the ever increasing wants of perpetually increasing fixed properties.

If "production," by the existence of a true law of money, *created demand*, then thought and wealth would be generally united in contra-distinction to small mental capacity and small income; nevertheless, under the true law, herein propounded, the most moderate ability would make a certain and comfortable living. The great majority of superior minds would make wealth, and the minority of of such would only fail in reaching their high aim because of positive faults of mental or physical organization; but would not descend to base poverty.

As all nations, with elective institutions, must rely for permanence on the virtue and intelligence of the citizens, I can not conceive the future of such nations under the present system of credit as the basis of production of material substances — which production I always adhere to as the "fundamental" of mankind's present, and the "nursery" of their future — without beholding a hereafter of moral degradation and social confusion, preceding a return to semi-barbarism and absolutism.

No wealth nor family types, under the credit law, can hope for perpetuation. All individual excellence, mental and physical, which, if wealth were always fully assured to talent and moral excellence, would be perpetuated, is now constantly drifted back into the baser and less advanced levels of human growth. Nothing short of the fierce power of strong men, in early states of society, supported afterwards by legislative enactments, has been able to secure any chance of descent of family types. But under unshackled production, which can only be through a true money, all families will be noble, and supported by wealth, who possess high intellectual and moral attributes; and, as these are generally accompanied by true physical conditions, a superior race of mankind, in all points of view, will be certain, and family descents, in distinct channels, will be as numerous as the trees in the forest.

Dupater, a French philosopher, is said to have exclaimed that "in the physical man the great moral mystery lies concealed." In the production of material substances (if under a sound law) will that "moral mystery" be brought forth and cultivated, taught to think, to feel, to see and to understand nature and nature's God.

Elihu Burritt, in his benevolence, sought to cheapen postage between the nations—England subsidizes mail packets—individuals form charity hospitals, and so forth—Legislatures pass relief laws for debtors, and protecting laws for creditors. This is all mere puny cobbling on a false fundamental system of human life. Within the law of unshackled production there will be no poor, no debtors, no creditors. Thought will be far more generally diffused, and man will then hold a position of individual freedom.

There is no man really free under the present system which governs production. It is not intended by nature that in forming nations the individual should lose his individuality; but he has, and it never can be restored until production is unshackled, and debtor and creditor unknown terms.

Under the present system all profits go into properties, such as farms, houses, machinery; and why? Because the world has never yet had a money channel where any portion of net profits can be permanently planted as money.

Thus all production resolves its profits into "properties," to be afterwards moved by a credit. Every thing called money, issued by Banks or Governments, is mere credit. Gold is not money, and there is only enough of it to form a "measure" of money. All the gold held by banks in "rest," is neither money nor the "evidences" of money. It is mere bullion, held by banks as a contingent against losses on their loans, and to create a species of confidence towards gaining a public credit for their "promises to pay" and deposits.

Gold is unqualified to become a money "evidence," from its limitations in quantity, and because of its fluctuating, merchantable character. Money, itself, is an invisible substance, emanating under a true law, however, from the net profits previously earned in the production of material substances.

A natural money is only limited by the amount of net profits requiring it, and by the amount that fixed properties can absorb in creating further production with the same.

A natural money needs no redemption, but should continue always growing, as the producing properties increase, and should be intrinsically valuable, by being indoctrinated in every value of the whole nation, inasmuch as all properties are dependent on it for their value, and have had a full "measure" of the money in gold expended in their behalf, and been increased in value to the extent of the money motor supplied, and of the sum not drawn away by taxation and tariffs.

The boundary of all nations is naturally designed to fall within the convenient evolutions of the industrial economy, and the expenses of a government naturally required to protect the property to be acquired, and the citizen while acquiring and enjoying the same, form the highway of nature, for the creation of a true money. Without this common necessity for a government, and the expenses of governing, there would be no way to make a true money of a universal value within a nation, and of unquestioned reliability in all the world.

Credit is a false money, be it in Bank, Government or Individual notes; it all rests on the profits *yet* to be made, and not, like a true money, on the profits *already earned.*

Credit is therefore unsteady, unsafe, limited, expensive, and it requires the half of each day of man's life to obtain it—to manage it, and to pay it. It makes all fixed property too cheap, and all productions too dear. It makes, also, too much of the former, and too little of the latter, under its system, but as compared with the rule of a true money and unshackled production, far too little of both.

Money that does not arise out of the net profits of production never fuses into the industry of the nation; it can not be evenly obtained to move production. It never goes into the saw-mill, the farm, the workshop, the village, the town, the city, to-day, where profits were made yesterday. And all men—farmers, mechanics, manufacturers—although making profits daily, are poor in money to move further production. Thus, under this false system, *demand* only creates, and at the same time LIMITS production, and this "limit" it is which originates what the clergy call the "wrath of God," for it covers the earth with sorrow and anguish, wretchedness and despair.

A true money, arising out of the net profits of yesterday, will be found through the local banker, in the very workshop or farm to-day, where it was earned, stimulating more and more production. It will cost no interest or any time to obtain it, it will ensure cheapened production and money sales for every thing. It will produce money and properties relatively equal, and multiply the productions and the fixed properties, hundreds-fold beyond the power of the present system. Under a true money and unshackled production, *production will create demand.* Every thing will then be sold that can be made; too much can not be made, and cash transactions will be universal. And this "unlimit" will remove that same "wrath of God" from off the face of the earth for ever.

The processes of life, advanced by Adam Smith and his successors, have made most things ready to hand, such as values, exchanges and so forth, therefore nothing is required of me but to proclaim the process of a true money; and it will, if adopted, step into life silently and unobtrusively, assimulating with all the rules of life and machinery of business now extant, and yet within TEN YEARS all debts of Individuals and of Governments, no matter how large, and interest on money, will be extinct. The Government debts having been paid in gold, the supply and demand of money will then be equal to meeting every transaction where credit now is necessary. Taxation will cease at once with the adoption of this law, inasmuch as the gold rolled into the bureau of production will far exceed the expenses of the chief Government, from the very first application of the law. Tariffs, which are merely indications of an incapable system of production, may depart at once, as far as Revenue is concerned; and in policy (?) as gradually as credit disappears, for with a full money in supply and demand equal, no one country can undersell another, unless from superior intellectuality applied to production. Unshackled production, to be so, needs a true money, but the full economy of the nation requires also untrammeled commerce, free goods and no navigation laws.

With the incubus of a false system removed, mankind under the benign influence of unshackled production, and as credit and its offspring, debt, disappear, and a full money advances, will see poverty growing less and less; and will feel the spirit of truth gradually dawning upon the long period of darkness that has heretofore shrouded their understandings; and the spiritual man will step forth, to be no more enslaved by the bondage of material transactions. The individual will then have his individuality intact. He will be a law unto himself, and will work out his own truths and his own salvation.

Then, there will be no more "poor," and less disease and crime; but there will be great general happiness and much increased length of days. Men will stay longer in business, because it will be safe and pleasant to do so.

When production creates demand, the conception of a real earnest *present*, full of purposes to God and man, clothed in justice, benevolence and truth, will dawn upon the world, and man will see God face to face, instead of imagining Him in or behind the clouds. And it may arise, that the teachings and example of Jesus Christ will then be comprehended as indicating, between the present and the future, a harmony which human reason will understand, believe, and act upon.

I confine myself, mostly, to pronouncing what is the true law of money, but while I rest with that, I could easily and satisfactorily explain and prove, how all affairs, including foreign exchange and transactions, will be subsidiary to, and be regulated by, the great domestic wheel whose axis is in the bureau of production. Should any nation adopt this system, and the others did not, then that nation would undersell the world, and exchange would be most extensively in its favor. But when all the nations of the world adopt the natural law of money, as I trust they all will, sooner or later, and the basis of all transactions being then ready money, then the foreign exchanges will be a mere secondary affair. No present banking system, or its issues, will be legally disturbed; their notes will be gradually displaced under the new system and new money. All natural laws are conservative, and the best test of the soundness of the law which I advance is that every person and every kind of transaction in life will be benefited by it. Truly understood, natural laws do not pull down—they build up!

Wars, plagues, famines are but trifles in their effects and results as compared with the slavery of credit and the debasement of debt.

Debt in every shape, from a bar of soap to millions in government stocks or railway bonds, is abhorrent to the natural law of production; and mortgages on fixed properties, when general, as they are in the United States and Canadas, indicate the last round of the ladder in the career of credit here, as the fearful pauperism of Europe forewarns the end of the credit system there.

As debt increases, the productions of labor decrease in profitability; but as debt decreases the production of material substances, and of all other occupations, multiply in quantity and in profit, to the extent of debt discharged, by triple over triple, onward.

There can be no indebtedness created by a nation so

large but that there must be productive power in the nation equal to discharging it. So long as debt weighs upon production, through tariffs, taxation and credit money, production can not rise to the power of rescuing itself. Hence we see population thrown out of work, poorhouses filled, brains stagnated and the moral man petrified.

Debt is unnecessary and unprofitable, originating out of the imperfect knowledge of how to apply floating and fixed capital to their relative conditions and proportions. It has not only desolated the human happiness and economy of three-fourths of mankind, for centuries, but has latterly, from its greater force and energy, deteriorated so much, through descent, the material organism of the brain, that intense selfishness and unrefined passions predominate to bar the door on high moral intellectuality in all matters bearing upon the amelioration, or refining, of the condition of mankind.

Men, with destructiveness, secretiveness and acquisitiveness large, and with adhesiveness, concentrativeness, conscientiousness and benevolence moderate, no matter how strong their intellectual organs, will not see the truth in this essay. It is not necessary that all men should. It is to be hoped that some will, who have power to sway legislation, and then, when this law is operative, it will rain its blessings on all alike, rich and poor, good and bad, wise and foolish.

Nature laid the foundation, Adam Smith and his successors built the columns, and, I believe, it has been given to me to place the keystone in the arch of Political Economy. This assumption of mine may sound like a boast. I do not mean it as such, but being convinced myself, I place my *light* on a high elevation, that it may be seen of all men, and only be extinguished by a new and greater light. Any attempt to discredit, by appeal to the present unintellectual hotch-potch system of temporary expediencies of the credit system, upon which life is certainly not moving upwards, will be no argument, but merely the dull animal assertions of *non-thought*.

The laws of nature are beneficent, and a system where ignorance, misery, poverty and sin are the rule, and where wisdom and understanding, happiness, wealth and virtue are the exceptions, forms no foundation for argument against a declaration of TRUTH.

www.ingramcontent.com/pod-product-compliance
Lightning Source LLC
Chambersburg PA
CBHW021556270326
41931CB00009B/1241